WRITING

IN THE

DARK

OTHER BOOKS BY MARTIN LOWENTHAL

Buddha and the Art of Intimacy

Alchemy of the Soul

Dawning of Clear Light

Embrace Yes

Heat to Heart, Hand in Hand, Shoulder to Shoulder

Opening the Heart of Compassion
(co-authored with Lar Short)

WRITING
IN THE
DARK

unseen poems

Martin Lowenthal

Dedicated Life Publications

Published in the United States by

Dedicated Life Publications

Printed by BookSurge

ISBN: 1-4392-5098-7

Cover and book design by Grace E. Pedalino
"Lotus" cover photo by Grace E. Pedalino

CONTENTS

Preface

Writing in the dark

Writing in the dark
does not offer the usual poetic images,
the angle of the sun through tree branches,
a squirrel chasing a squirrel
along the top of a picket fence,
or the white orchid on the kitchen table.
The endless black merits
hardly an obvious comment.
The impulse to create, however, is quite notable.

These poems are dedicated to the creative spirit that inspired them. Writing has become a practice in the numerous dark retreats that I have done over the past sixteen years. A dark retreat involves living in total darkness. I have done seventeen dark retreats to date, generally for two week and as long as one month.

Over the years of doing these retreats, I have developed a method for physically writing in the dark* and a discipline for crafting poems that I could not see. The poems in this collection were written in dark retreats in 1998, 2001, 2003, 2004, 2005, 2006, 2007, 2008 and 2009.

*A METHOD FOR WRITING IN THE DARK: The method I developed for writing is quite simple. I take a pad of 5x8 paper. I place the index finger of my left hand on the left edge of the pad to mark where I have begun a line. I write across the page and upon reaching the right edge, my left index finger moves down. I find it with my pen and begin another line. If my lines are shorter than the width of the page, I simply move my finger down and begin a new line. I put each written page at the back of the pad whenever I reach the bottom, decide to pause in my writing, or have completed a poem. I have written hundreds of pages of journals, poems, and stories in the dark.

Love

When I Saw You

The moment I saw you
I fell into eternity.
Magically my heart opened
to catch my fall.

When I saw you
a silent cry of longing
broke out of its secret prison.

When I saw you
a single tear sealed my surrender.

When I saw you
my heart went one way
and my head went another.

My mind was lost for weeks
while my heart danced
through the nights and days
intoxicated with the wine of love.

When they met up again some time later,
my heart had to teach my untrained mind
how to abandon its sober ways.

Inside

Inside this union,
there is no inner and outer,
only love.

Inside the sacred,
there is no inner and outer,
only the Divine.

Inside life,
there is no inner and outer,
only creation.

Outside these
there is homelessness, desperation and numbness.
Inside these,
is the rapture that was always desired.

Hidden Bird

A hidden bird lives
inside my being.
It was quiet and still,
until I met You.

Now it sings, sings, sings,
and flies, flies, flies,
and is making a nest for You
in my heart.

The Heavens

Your crescent moon smile
turns your eyes into stars.

Every now and then
I dive into water
and float on the river of memory
that opens into the ocean of You.

Your smile is the hearth of dawn.
Your embrace is the hearth of night.

My kisses and caresses
        are the gentle waves
        at the shore of your being
conveying the fullness and depth
        of the ocean of my love.

The Worshipper

My body worships
at the temple of your passion
that turns your nipples into firm sweet raisins
and makes nectar flow from the well of your
desire.

Heart at Home

My heart, not satisfied with the company of other organs,
gathers family, friends, lovers,
children, and assorted strangers
in its embrace.

How wondrous that it leaves with so many
and remains home with me.

Mis-under-standing

"You don't understand me or you would know
what I want."
"How can I understand you unless you say what
you want?"
And so it goes,
as the dog slides between them
and each reaches out in ways
that have been repeated hundreds of times,
one behind the ears
the other to the wiggling rump.
The dog thinks
understanding doesn't hold a candle to
good strokes in the right places.

An Incomparable Love Poem

I don't know how turning you into a simile
became associated with being poetic.

Beautiful images such as
roses, oceans, and stars
have been trivialized by Hallmark
and do not hold up to scrutiny.

Roses get afflicted by insects and wither,
oceans have sharks and pollution,
and the stars are so distant
it would take more than my lifetime to reach them.

But I suppose, given your tastes,
you might be a fine meal
and together we make up a stew
that becomes more flavorful
over time
on a steady flame.

The Dancers

They waltz around the floor
like two hippos.
Other dancers turn their attention
out of caution and amusement.
They see heavenly grace expressed
on the two blissful faces
evoking smiles of joy that fill the room.

Love Poem for the Divine

You are embracing love,
radiant, pervasive, luminous,
sweet and sticky like honey.

In your omnipresence
You are the fragrance of the rose,
as well as the fart,
the pleasure of orgasm
and the pain of loss,
the caress of the breeze
and the power of the hurricane.

You are the lover
that loves everyone else as well.

My love affair with you
attacks my ego
and I feel abandoned
by the way your world treats me.

Even as I know,
from this relationship
there is no escape.

Body of My Beloved

Beloved, your generous body
caresses all in the vibrant stillness of night.
Your naked beauty is revealed at dawn
and lovers are invited
to drink from your well
and immerse in your flowing river.
Your mountains rise majestically
above your fertile valley.

There are some
who shrink from your embrace
and would cover your magnificence
with robes of judgment and righteousness.
But Eros will not remain hidden
and the fierce challenges of life
can only be met
in the name of true love.

The Chain

Compassion is a chain of connection.
Heartache is its lock
and the bond is pure love.

Dark Retreat Life and Practice

Freedom and Sight

Living in a small, completely dark room,
my mind is emancipated
from the bondage of bills, correspondence,
petty conversations, and entertainment.

My attention expands into vast space,
dancing to the tune of presence.
My soul luxuriates in recreative preparation
to once again see the sky, feed the birds,
kiss my wife, play hide and seek, and share stories.

Light and darkness each have a price,
and I willingly pay each its due.

Beyond Ordinary

Living in darkness reverses everything.
I see visions invisible to the eye,
listen to silence inaudible to the ears,

sense presences the body cannot touch
and abide in clear light
that is normally obscured.

Luminous Silence

In this retreat of total darkness
radiant consciousness
that has been hidden in the shadows
rises above the horizon of distraction
and illuminates the silence.

Thoughts pause to marvel in awe.
The heart sighs at being home.
The vastness of space resounds with quiet joy.

Some lights are only seen in darkness,
some songs only heard in silence,
great forces only felt in stillness,
and our true longing only known
in the absence of desire.

Assault

In this dark place
stillness surrounds the body.

Silence pierces
the heart of habitual thinking.

The wound to the mind
is clarity.

Illumination

The full moon illuminates entire landscapes
and the dark retreat remains beyond its reach.

Yet the full light of clarity
fills the room and all space.

Here and Now in Dark Retreat

When we open our eyes in light,
we go from inside to the outside world
of form, shape, size and position
and time is marked by moving from here to there.

In this black cave,
here opens to the boundless
and now is defined
by pervasive presence.

I sit in the stony silence of the dark
penetrating the black with wide eyes.
Lights flash from nowhere,
reds, greens and blues
pulse at my naked vision.

My skin touches and is touched by the vibrating air.
My heart senses a world,
vast beyond imagination.
I cannot tell where I begin or end
or whether this is my experience
or the sigh of an unknown presence.

The Offer

The woman sitting next to me
offers to transcribe and print out
my poems while I continue to meditate.

I think what a wonderful offer.
Then I could review and share them for feedback.

I realize that I cannot see
which sheets of scribbled paper have poems on them.
I am in dark retreat.

Furthermore, she does not exist.
I am dreaming.

My lucidity punctures the dream of support
as I sleep in my solitary womb of darkness.

Sunrise in Dark Retreat

As the sun of conscious memory rises
          above the horizon of slumber,
It brings the objects of my world back into being—
          bed, night stand, cushion.
In this room of darkest night,
          there is no need of shadows.

Terrain of the Dark

Maps and eyesight are useless
in the terrain of the dark.
Only the perceptions of a sacred heart
can behold the vast intimacy
of this primal landscape.

Great Darkness

Great Darkness opens and invites
the loving, fierce penetration of Extreme Light

and her womb forever carries
the visions of possibility.

The universe never sleeps again.

Darkness

Darkness absorbs everything,
     light, sounds, tears, pain, songs
and all words and images ever made
     into its infinity.

Only the Clear Light of Divine Awareness
     comprehends its magnitude
and only the unconditional presence of a loving heart
     can apprehend its magnificence.

At Home in the Dark

It is only in the dark that I am reminded
        of how blind I am in daily light.
It is through feeling water
in the unseen space of my retreat room
        that I am struck by the miracle of small things.
In the song of the birds outside,
        the fragrance of cooked rice,
the mind releases its claim to the attention of the heart
        as I open to what is.

Nothing is held beyond the moment.
Judgments and comments give way to presence.
Thundering silence and dynamic stillness
        energize my heart posture of praise.
This eternal moment of resounding joy
        simply serves the delicious glory
        of the taste of cool, fresh water in a dark home.

Sitting in the Dark

Sitting on a firm cushion, thoughts come and go
        mind remains.
Feelings arrive insistently and exit reluctantly,
        heart remains.
Inner lights and colors arise, pass through and disappear,
        darkness remains.
"I" goes
        "Am" remains.

Daily Life and Celebrations

Music of the Day

The Hallelujah chorus of birds
accompanies the sunrise.
At sunset they sing
a requiem for the day.

Finn and The Bite of Salmon*

With one taste of king salmon,
blasts of delight assault my palate,
awakening my senses,
inflaming my soul,
consuming my body,
leaving the aftertaste of Grace.

*Finn MacCool, the legendary chieftain of the *fienna* in
Ireland, who gained his wisdom from eating a salmon.

As teeth crush a grape,
the palate sings a sweet melody.
Every cell, even hairs,
sigh in praise.

The Bath

My pleasure loving skin
delights in the
caresses and embrace of the bath.

I marvel that my body
does not follow the water
down the drain.

Pausing on a path in the wild woods,
I can almost hear the carpenter's song
the ants sing to
a fallen log
as they recycle its life
as a tree
into a home.

She ambles fearless
across the yard
in all her splendid furriness,

pauses to gaze through the dim morning light
at the mildly alarmed meditator
then leisurely lumbers to the woods
wagging her skunky tail.

Traces

The cardinal glides over the snowy ground
making no tracks
yet leaving traces of beauty
in my memory.

Dandelion

The keepers of lawnscape propriety
see an unwelcome erection
amid crew-cut fur.

To lovers of wild beauty
this golden offering of head
seeks to pleasure the sky.

Snow kisses trees, rocks, ground
   and myself
      with silent abandon,
          enfolding all in its cold, loving embrace,

  knowing that its
     passion for earth
       will end
           in its utter dissolution.

Night Goddess

The fading radiance of day
sinks into the bosom of the Night Goddess
as she adorns herself with stars

a brush stroke of cloud
a pendant moon to entrance
enticing the eyes of wonder.

Night is the Temple

Night is the temple
the flowers fold their petals
and bow their heads
as the breeze fills the world
with the fragrance of prayer.

Shadows

In the brilliance of full moon night,
willow and oak
cast dappled and feathery shadows,
leaving footprints of wonder and beauty
in the ground of memory.

Each day, like early spring,
the seeds of my longing
push through thawing ground,
impelled by the possibility of light
and new blossoming.

Daily Service

In the temple of my heart
the service has no sermon or announcements

only hymns of longing, praise and love
and the Sabbath lasts all week.

Rhythms of Passover

The service, once led by my grandfather
just as his father had done and
as my uncle after,
I do now, again and again.

Each night we become free from bondage.
Each generation, each year, each moment,
reiterates the rhythm of enslavement and liberation.

Longing for an end
we miss the playing

Life says, there is no beginning
so no end,
just the play it again.

One

I live as though I am The One.
Yet I see a world
filled with people convinced
that they are The One.

I know that thinking I am The One
prevents me from being One,
experiencing ultimate Oneness.

I work on becoming no one,
so I can attain being One
thus being the One
who is One.

Becoming too preoccupied
with one self
gets one stuck
in duality.

Embarrassing Moments

Embarrassing moments have been
among my most effective teachers.
They have never been repeated.

At age four, I explained to my skeptical parents
why I was late coming home from playing in the woods,
because a giant tomato and a gnarly carrot
decided to block the trail
and refused to let me pass.

Or, when I told Janey,
a beautiful activities director,
that when I grew up in fifteen years
I would marry her,
not knowing she was already engaged
to Mike, the camp director.

Or, the time I took a dump in my pants
and pretended to the rest of my first grade class
that the smell must be coming from Tommy Smaltz.

Or, the time I sang solo in a junior high school show
in a key no one had ever heard before.

Or, being seen on a date with Debbie
by Martha with whom I had a date
later the same evening.

It may be that my life has been propelled
by a series of obvious mistakes.

Following Memories

Like other nights I follow memories of you into sleep.
In dream you are transformed
        into a model in an art class at the Louvre.
After class, you dress and we walk into a barn
        where you struggle to get the hang of
        the pull and squeeze on the udder
        of a cow who keeps
        looking around perplexed about
        what has happened to the milkmaid.
Frustrated, we leave and enter a tavern
        in Barcelona where you become a wild gypsy dancer
        and we go out into the night to sing to the moon.
In the morning, I follow memories of you
        into the day, wondering
        who you are now.

Celebration

Suddenly, in the midst of a peaceful meditation, Your presence swept through and around my body. Bright light filled my vision. I became naked and bathed in the river of that love. Even the little hairs on my arms stood up and rejoiced.

Zafu, The Guru

Who would have guessed that
    such a lofty teacher
    would occupy such a lowly position.

Pressed into service,
    the cushion unconditionally supports
    all manner and sizes of posteriors.

It receives with utter equanimity
    the foul winds that practitioners pass.

Its stability of purpose
    goes unacknowledged at the end of sitting
    as it is placed unceremoniously
    into a heap to patiently rest, cheek to cheek,
    with the other stuffy teachers.

And when, after years of endless end-full service,
    the threads of its current form dissolve,
    it surrenders completely, not knowing
what new incarnation will be its contribution,
    what new, higher purpose it may be given
    after kissing us so lovingly.

Tears of Grief

Tears of grief
do not obscure my vision.
Rather, they cleanse the eyes of my heart
to more clearly view
an interior landscape of love
that is no longer beheld
in the visible world.

Remembering My Mother

She would be turning 98 this year.
I am comforted that
she did not live this long.

I would see her now
bent over from osteoporosis,
        head straining to make eye contact,
her descended organs
        piled upon each other
        at her waist.

I would have to watch
her pain and discomfort
overwhelm her fragile tolerance.

It is better that I remember her
on our last visit,
her mind still sharp,
her body somewhat tentative
yet functioning to support her insistent interest
in learning, her loving nature,
and her delight in simple pleasures.

Her life, though challenging, was still rich.
She even talked about dying with grateful vitality
days before her fatal accident nine years ago.

Clearing the Basement

In preparing the family house for a new owner
and a fresh vision,
I sort through boxes filled with old memories.
Some reform with easy recall.
And others collapse,
disintegrated by the termites of time.

I grieve them both
as I clear out an old home,
feeling surprisingly lighter
belonging more fully to the present.

Limping

Each day we struggle awkwardly with the infirmity
         of long suffered wounds and weaknesses
         moving with a magnificent, determined limp
         to our destination.

We light a candle of hope for peace.
Then our own anger blows it out.

The tear of a father whose daughter
        perished on September 11,
The kaddish of a youth whose parents
        died on a bus bombed in Jerusalem,
The grief cry of a Palestinian mother on hearing of
        her son's death in the Intifada,
The famine-hollowed faces of
        mother, father, and child in southern Sudan,
The secret chants of monks
        imprisoned in slave labor camps in Tibet,
All these are seen, heard, and felt more clearly in the
dark and silence of retreat
        than in the light and noise of busy life.

Enough

There are not enough tears in the eyes and the heart
	for the enormity of the world's pain.
There is not enough respect in our minds
	for the strength and dignity of the human spirit.
There is not enough praise on tongues
	for the wonder, awe, and grace of the Divine.

Yet when we offer ourselves wholeheartedly
	in the service of life, love and beauty,
	it is always enough.

Avalokiteshvara* drops two tears in my eyes
to see the pain in the world.
The river of grief carves great canyons in my heart
to hold it all
and still there is more.
Yet the beauty of those vast wounds
transforms everything
into the boundless radiance of an open landscape.

*Avalokiteshvara is a Buddhist deity of compassion.

An Outlaw Koan

Two robbers, unknown to each other, enter the bank lobby from separate doorways. Taking out their guns, they simultaneously shout, "Put up your hands, give me all your money or die!"

Who lives?

The Laugh in a Meditation Hall

A blast of delight
to awaken slumbering serious seekers.

On Listening to Isaac Stern

Violinist and violin sway in union
in the key of love.
A seed is planted in my heart
that grows with every note.
Ascending to the heart of heaven
on the silk thread of a
Mendelssohn concerto,
my life on earth is ablaze
with sacred passion.

A Great Idea

A great idea stands lonely
       among a crowd of pedestrian thoughts.
It longs for immortality.
Its great fear is not doubt
      or contradiction;
It is being forgotten.

The Altar

The water offering longs
       to return to its flowing source.
The blossoms wait
       to rot in mother earth.
The flame dances
       until it returns home to darkness.

Fiery Gold

The fiery gold of sunrise
awakens the soul
planting seeds of the day.

The fiery gold of sunset
melts the heart into honey
to be harvested by the night lover.

Playground of Awareness

The warrior of consciousness,
awakened after centuries of waiting,
draws her radiant sword of attention,
cutting thoughts into silence.

Other thoughts come forward and retreat
and confusion folds in on itself,
as the mind settles
into the open landscape of clarity.

The Trouble with Meditation Practice

Seated on my cushion,
I contemplate the foolishness of practice.

What am I rehearsing for?
Am I counting breaths
to become proficient at counting
so I can enter a breathing competition?

Just when I have thought
all the thoughts I have to think,
the attainment of no-thought is marred
by the mental comment
on the pleasure of achieving no-thought.

Can I really practice no-self?
Is this all preparation for a command performance
at which "I" am a no-show?

Who Are You

(based on the poem *Lost* by David Wagoner)

Be still. The air you breathe and the sounds you hear
Are not confused. Who you are is Here and Now,
And you must treat it as a powerful stranger,
Must open wholeheartedly to know it and be known.
Listen. The surf of silence, it answers,
"I have made this world around you,
If you leave, you may come home again by simply attending."
No two sensations are the same to the body.
No two moments are the same in experience.
If what a sensation or a moment does is lost on you,
You are surely lost. Be still. The silence knows
Who you are. You must let it define you.

A Traveling Companion

Long ago I joined others on the path of wisdom.
Over time I have learned a little.
Those who think they know,
        don't.
Those who think they do not know,
        don't.
Those who have come to love the journey,
        have a chance.

Wisdom is supremely selective.
She cannot be gained or captured
        as a prize to be won.
She chooses who
        she will walk beside
as an unseen, silent
        and loving companion.

Sword of Inquiry

The sword of inquiry
attacks relentlessly with the chant
"who am I?"

until the mind consumes
itself and forgets that it once
was somebody.

Writing about Meditation

Writing poetry or anything
about meditation
is to elaborate at length
about essentially nothing.

The Relative

Nothing can be said about the absolute.
What can be said about the relative,
depends.
It's in the eye of the beholder.
Like the snail who was mugged
by a turtle and couldn't say
what happened because
it all went by so fast.
Or, the driver on a freeway
who hears on the radio
that a nut is driving the wrong way
on the freeway.
He thinks "One nut? Hell.
I'm facing hundreds of them."

Perspectives may be relative
but life always means relationship
not by comparison
but by interconnection and interbeing.
Each is a feature of what is,
not what isn't.
What is,
is a change from the viewpoint
of what was.
Since nothing persists
what is,
is always what is,
forever.

Essentially "I" do not exist.
Existentially I do exist.
Essentially "I" am out of it.
Existentially I am stuck in it.
Some say "such is life."
I say,
"Let's dance."

Echoes

My experiences echo
in the canyon of thoughts
and I cannot help listening
to the hollow repetitions
as if they matter.

"Stop that!" I say
to my mind,
and frustration echoes in
diminishing cycles.

I pause,
listen to the silence.

"Ah ha!" I say triumphantly.
"Ah ha!" "Ah ha!" "Ah ha!" "Ah ha!" "Ah ha!"

The Swing

A glimpse led to a touch
and then a kiss
and momentary union.
I am now a servant
of the Divine.
I ride the great swing
that moves between
the superficial and the sacred
embracing the realization
that I may swing back and forth
forever.

The Mirror

Haven't you ever been suspicious
of the mirror as a metaphor
for the nature of mind?

I can imagine that in impulsive moments
of personal expression, my mirror sticks out
a tongue as soon as I turn away.
And just as quickly, if I turn back,
it assumes its faithful, unshakable reflection.

My mind, on the other hand,
will make unseemly and laughable faces
whether I am watching or not.
Even the mind that notices
gives a snicker now and then.

The Hound

By some gastronomic clock
around the same hour each day,
A not so subtle split occurs.

While my mind abides in spacious awareness,
a small part goes to sit by the door.
Riding the edge of patience and salivation,
this hound nature draws more and more attention
away from the nature of mind.

When the dinner knock comes,
a nearly ravenous beast
is ready to pounce
when the way is clear.

With a willing shrug,
my consciousness joins the feast
surrendering to the radiance of taste,
delighting in the play of natures.

Global Mind

What a wonder—
the wandering mind

       that can traverse the globe to China,
       discourse on world events,
       and plan the coming month,

misses the caress
of the breeze on my cheek.

Bell of Compassion

Wood strikes metal.
We resonate in the world of its ringing scream,
opened by the tear in silence.

Insights

Attention is the dagger
consciousness makes
when its point strikes the moment
cutting the skin of distraction
and opening the way for presence.

Light

A beam of clarity
          at the heart of any insight.

Our longing for God
may be strong,
but an often stronger desire
is to become
someone else's God.

Religious Conversion

In the temple of thought
everything is converted into words.
On the sacred way
words are converted into pavers
making a passage to ecstasy.

The heart in our words
turns the conversation
into an ecstatic dance
on a giant lotus blossom.

Tears can feed
a pool of bitterness
or water the tree of love.
Cultivate the garden
that has been entrusted to you.

Narcissism and its attendant
addictions, fears, and onanism
make the soul small
and the Sacred distant.

Light is the womb of day,
darkness the womb of night,
and Love the womb of life.

Being Inside

Ah, poet, it does not interest me
to know what is inside you.
Share what it means to be inside life
and what it feels like to be inside God.
Then we can bridge the gap between us.

Memories

Memories are not always pathways
        into the past.
Some are stories displayed
        on the coffee table at gatherings.
Others are the recitation of wounds
        in the dungeons of anger and hate.
And still others are passages in a hymnal of praise
        sung in the temple of belonging.

Tears

Don't wipe away tears
to keep this world in focus.
They are a lens
into the landscape of the heart
and a nectar of the soul.

Thought

Experience casts its thoughts.
Even the epiphany of high noon
gives way to afternoon shadows.

We write stories of our past in the air
while the thirsty earth of our soul
waits for the blood, sweat, and tears of Now
so something beautiful can grow.

Open wounds are not ever-present.
They are re-inflicted by constant recall.

Scars, on the other hand,
make up the contours of our beauty.

Self-Righteousness

the angry offspring
  of frustrated disappointment
  and primal fear
costumed in priestly garb.

Cloak of Prayer

We fashion a cloak of prayer
with images made of words,
emblazoned with the color of feeling
and threaded with songs rooted in longing,
all woven into the fabric of silence.

This mysterious cape protects
by making us transparent,
revealing our hidden heart to the invisible Divine.

THE DEDICATED LIFE INSTITUTE (DLI) supports spiritual exploration and growth and is dedicated to making the essence teachings of many traditions accessible in a Western idiom. Incorporating the principles of the mystic way, we promote both recovery of our wisdom ground of being and development of our capacity to use our daily conditions as a means of growth and the opportunity to manifest our true wisdom and loving nature. Our dedication to living as an expression of wisdom and love serves to encourage both personal and social transformation. The Institute offers meditation groups, retreats, workshops, and a home study program. For more information please visit our website at www.dli.org.

3965382

Made in the USA